SOUTH CAROLINA PAPERS

Other Heritage Books by Craig L. Heath:

*Georgia, Alabama and South Carolina Papers
Volume 1V of the Draper Manuscript Collection*

South Carolina Papers, Volume 1TT of the Draper Manuscript Collection

The George M. Bedinger Papers in the Draper Manuscript Collection

The Illinois Manuscripts, Volume 1Z of the Draper Manuscript Collection

The Mecklenburg Declaration

The Virginia Papers, Volume 1, Volume 1ZZ of the Draper Manuscript Collection

The Virginia Papers, Volume 2, Volume 2ZZ of the Draper Manuscript Collection

The Virginia Papers, Volume 3, Volume 3ZZ of the Draper Manuscript Collection

The Virginia Papers, Volume 4, Volume 4ZZ of the Draper Manuscript Collection

The Virginia Papers, Volume 5, Volume 5ZZ of the Draper Manuscript Collection

SOUTH CAROLINA PAPERS

Volume 1TT
of the
Draper Manuscript
Collection

Transcribed and Indexed by
Craig L. Heath

HERITAGE BOOKS
2011

HERITAGE BOOKS

AN IMPRINT OF HERITAGE BOOKS, INC.

Books, CDs, and more—Worldwide

For our listing of thousands of titles see our website
at
www.HeritageBooks.com

Published 2011 by
HERITAGE BOOKS, INC.
Publishing Division
100 Railroad Ave. #104
Westminster, Maryland 21157

International Standard Book Numbers
Paperbound: 978-0-7884-3288-0
Clothbound: 978-0-7884-8787-3

INTRODUCTION

Volume 1TT of the *Draper Manuscripts* consists of: (1) an agreement, dated May 3, 1781, for exchange of American soldiers held prisoner by the British at Charleston, S. C., with British prisoners held by the American forces at Jamestown, Va.; (2) a list of the American officers held prisoner at Charleston; (3) an account book kept by the Clark family in 1777-78; and (4) muster rolls of Capt. Harman Davis's company of South Carolina artillery (1778-79).

This transcription of the *Virginia Papers* was made from the 1980 microfilm edition of the Draper Manuscripts, Volume 1TT. Portions of the documents in this volume are illegible or poorly legible, owing to fading, staining, discoloration, or disintegration of the paper with loss of parts of pages. Where illegible, these portions (whether single words or entire passages) are indicated by ellipses (...); some effort has been made to interpret poorly legible portions, but the original manuscript or microfilm copy should be consulted for verification. The spelling, punctuation, capitalization, and grammar used in the original documents have been preserved so far as feasible. The transcript should be viewed as an aid to use of the manuscript, rather than a replacement or substitute for it, and users are urged to consult the original manuscript or the microfilm in parallel with the transcript.

Page numbers are handwritten on the pages of the original manuscript. These are indicated in brackets at the beginning of each page in the transcript. Owing to the variability in length of text on the manuscript pages, no attempt has been made to correlate page breaks in the transcript with those in the manuscript. The pages of the account book are presented in this transcript in numerical order, although they were not microfilmed in numerical order.

The Draper Manuscripts are owned by the Wisconsin Historical Society; the cooperation of the Society in the production of this volume is hereby gratefully acknowledged.

VOLUME 1TT

[p. 1]

...th Carolina]

Cartel May 3d 1781 in S. C. <u>Prisoners</u>

...tecles of Cartel for the exchange & relief of the Prisoners of war taken in the southern department agreed to at the house of Mr. Claudeus Pigue on ... third of May 1781 between Capt. Cornwallis to the part of Liut. Genl. Cornwallis & Lieut. Colonel ...rington on the part of Majr. Genl. Green.

   Article ... had regula... be exchang'd for regular troops, ... for Militia.

   2d ... for six months & ... on state service

   3 ... exchange be ra... similar rank ...

[p. 2]

   4th Th... be exchanged by rotation according to the date ... captivity, but a reciprocal apli'd ... be exercised in the non Commission'd and privates, by naming particular ... or particular persons.

   5th That no non Commiss... or private soldier ... adm..., be consider'd as prisoner ... finally Liberated ... the faith of a ...

   ...fficers that ...s'd for wan... to apply, ...ld to them ... exchanged

[p. 3]

subject to be recall'd for a breach thereof, or for a violation of the Cartel by the parties to which they belong.

   7th That passports be ...ow'd for such supplies as may be sent from either side to prisoners in Captivity.

   8th That Commissarys of prisoners be permitted to pass from each side into the opposite lines, and reside there for the purpose of viewing and representing the situation of the prisoners, but removable by the respective Commanding officers.

9th That prisoners shall not be sent from the Continent whilst the articles of Cartel continues to be observ'd.

10th That Commissarys ... prisoners shall immediat... put in practice such exchange on the above principles as far as the subjects on both sides will go and continue them in future as Characters shall apply.

11th That the first delivery of American prisoners shall embark at Charles Town on or before the 15th June & sail immediately for James Town in James

River where the first delivery of British prisoners shall embark for the nearest British post on or about the first week in July & sail Immediately.

12th That the flag of truce shall be sacred going with the American prisoners & returning with British to the post where they are to be deliver'd.

Officers prisoners of war Charles Town

Generals		Lt. Col.	
Moultre		Henderson	Ex.
McEntosh		Malem	Ex.
Woodford	Dead	Little [Archd. Lytle]	
Scott		Harney	
Hogan	Dead	Ball	
Colonels		Wallace	
Elbert		Decambrey	
Pinckney		Hopkins	
Russell		Cabell	Nevile
Gist		Clark	
Clark		Grimkey	
Delemoy		Vaughn	
Patten		Woolford	

Nevill
Heth
Beekman

[p. 7]

Majors		Captains	
Hogg	Ex	Cuthbert	Ex
Anderson	Ex	Hill	Ex
Debram	Ex	St. Maria	Ex
Habersham	Ex	McRee	Ex
Stephenson	Ex	Warley	Ex
Croghan		Smith	Ex
Nelson		Moseley	Ex
Waggoner		McTreevell	Ex
Harlston		Dickson	Ex
Lewis		Dandridge	Ex
Mitchell		Gillison	Ex
Pelham		Johnson	Ex
Lowe		Shelton	Ex
Pinckney		Milven	Ex
Windar		Heth	Ex
Pattan		Celeron	Ex

[p. 8]

Tatum	Ballard
Nash	Ingles
Turner	Murray
Coleman	Craddock
Mosick	Warley
Turner	Theebrich
Parker	Pain
Warley	Infant
Broozard	Elliott
Kinsbury	Dezeong
Booker	Baker

Thews   Pravaux
Goodwin   Heft
Blackwell   Kendal
Taliafero   Sommers
Day   Sinem

[p. 9]
Buchanan   Weekley
Bradly   Pollard
Baker   Minnis
Buckner   Wright
Gadsden   White
Mason   Mallaroy
Nevill   Edwards
Farrer   Curry
Little   Jackson
Grey   Cocke
Mounfort   Scriber
Holt   Cowen
Hite   Henley
Brackenridge   Lynch
Carrington   Brice
Butler   Morriss
Beale   Lamott
                             Hamilton

[p. 10]
Gaiway   Liuts
Smith   Wosham   Ex
Waters   Bradwell   Ex
Capt. Liuts   Dayley   Ex
Jones   Cowherd   Ex
Elliott   Castin   Ex
Gordett   kill'd   Barbey   Ex
Willson   Evins   Ex

Budd		Towns	Ex	
Stewart		Moss	Ex	
Terry		Decoyn	Ex	
Swearingham		Stubblefield	Ex	
Fitzgerrald		Minniss	Ex	
Porterfield		Walton	Ex	
Tate		Indom	Ex	
Kellender		Daves	Ex	
Alexander				
Waters				

[p. 11]

Becott	Ex	Hamilton	Ex
Parker	Ex	Johnson	Ex
Bowne	Ex	Vanduvall	Ex
Reed	Ex	Walker	Ex
Fox	Ex	Smith	Ex
Feeley	Ex	Cotgraves	Ex
Marshall	Ex	Morton	Ex
Budd	Ex	Brackinridge	Ex
McNease	Ex	Roth	Ex
Hart	Ex	Nelson	Ex
Roy	Ex	Jerrutt	
Blackwell	Ex	Goodwin	
Hog	Ex	Foisign	
Campaine	Ex	Hobb	
Mabern	Ex	Baskervill	
~~Callender~~		Lackford	
Clendennen	Ex	Feason	
		Moore	

[p. 12]

Plater	Shaw
Fryerson	Legras
Miller	Ward

Winchester		Pasteur	Ex Ag
Stark		Hazzard	
Merriwether		Grayson	
Liston		Brown	
Stevens		Tatum	
Allen		Ward	
White		Loyd	
Graves		Hays	
Vance		Dunbar	
Hamilton	Car	Hart	
Ogier		Hartgrave	
Evins		Stiche	
Moseley		Wallace	

[p. 13]

Mosely		Petree	
Purvis		Kennedy	
H Duff		Mazeek	
Harriss		Lowe	Dist
Reed		Thomas	
Harrison		Feash	Do
Norriss		Knapp	
		Jerdon	

2 Leiuts		Ensigns	
~~Eskridge~~	~~Ex~~	Eskridge	Ex
Russell	Ex	Fennce	Ex
Taliafero	Ex	Conway	Ex
Rooney	Ex	Holt	Ex
Norrell	Ex	Kennon	Ex
Kelly - Deserted to Eny.		Steel	Ex
McGuire	Ex	Robertson	Ex

[p. 14]

Jones	Ex	Cradock	Ex
Smith	Ex	Finnie	
Sladg	Ex	Gibson	
Ellhorn	Ex	Cruleher	
Brown	Ex	Heth	
Ford	Ex	Clark	
Ash	Ex	Roach	
Wallace	Ex	Linghton	
Rankins	Ex	W Williams	
Powell	Ex	Burges	
Miller	Ex	Gassaway	
Delaplain	Ex		
Heys	Ex		
Blackmore	Ex		

[p. 15]

<u>14</u>

1777	Contra	Crl.		
	By Cash		3	
	By do. 6 dollars			
	By 1 Bill of 10/		10	
	By 1 do. of 20/	1		
	By 43 lb. Beef			
	By 13 lb. do.			
	By 11 lb. do.			

[p. 16]

<u>14</u>

1777	John Huff	Dr.		
	To 1 Cow Hide to Mr. Sexton	1	16	
	To Cash paid Casper Rinker		6	
	To do. Paid John Lawrence	1	10	0

13

Contra	Cr.
Contra	Cr.
Contra	Cr.
Contra	Cr.
Contra	Cr.

13

| 1777 | Peter Steenbergen | Dr. |
| May 29 | To 3 Bags | |

1777   Edward Smith   Dr.
To 14 days Attendance & medcine of Doctr.}
      for negro Jack   }
Memdm. Mr. Smiths Team returnd July the 4th 1777

1777   John Adams   Dr.
To 4 Broad Bags   2 narrow do.

1777   John Patterson   Dr.
May 5 To 7 new Bags

1777   Jones Waggoner   Dr.
May 5 To 2 Broad Bags
      To 1 narrow do. Country Linen

12

| Contra | Cr. |

Contra   Cr.

Contra   Cr.

Contra   Cr.

Contra   Cr.

[p. 20]

<u>12</u>

1777	Samuel Lupton	Dr.			
May 16	To Cash paid for Hay		4	1	6

1777	Thomas Edmondson	Dr.
May 16	To 1 Sack Bag	

1777	William Holliday	Dr.
May 3	To 2 days Hauling	
June 4	to 4 days do.	

1777	James Hutchinson	Dr.
May 4	To 2 days Hawling	
June 4	To 2 days Do.	

1777	John Soniers	Dr.
June 29	To 1 Bag	

[p. 21]

<u>11</u>

Contra   Cr.

Contra   Cr.

Contra   Cr.

Contra   Cr.

Contra   Cr.

[p. 22]

11

| 1777 | Mr. Abernathy | Dr. |
| Apl. 13 | To 13 Bags | |

| 1777 | Robert Wilson | Dr. |
| Apl. 6 | To 4 lb. Mutton | |

| 1777 | Robert Page | Dr. |
| Apl. 6 | To 4 lb. Mutton by Patterson | |

| 1777 | James McCray | Dr. |
| Apl. 6 | To 4 Bags | |

| 1777 | James Gaml. Dondall | Dr. |
| May 3 | To Hawling 2 Load Planks | |

[p. 23]

10

Contra   Cr.

Contra   Cr.

Contra   Cr.

[p. 24]

10

1777	Colo. John Nevill	Dr.	
Apl. 9	To 3 Bushs. Corn	14th 3 Bushs. do.	
16	To 4 Bushs. do.		
21	To ½ Bushl. do. by Jas. Williams		

30	To 5½ do. at twice
May 14	To 1 Bushl. do.
16	To 4 Bushls. & 1 Bag p order
	To 1 do.
June 20	To 2 do. 1 pair Stockings

1777	John Rutter Dr.
Apl. 9	To 2 wide Bags & 1 narrow do.

1777	Mr. Bradford Dr.
May 3	To 1 Bag

[p. 25]

5   Cr.

By amount of Credit brought forwd.

[p. 26]

5   Dr.

1777	To Amount brought Forward
June 22	To 8 Bushs. Corn & 200wt. Hay to Ths. Murphy }
	returning from Pha. to Bedfd. County}
Sepr. 14	To Cash paid Peter Dick Junr. for}
	12 Bushs. Wheat @ 7/6 } 4 10 0
	To 2 Bushs. Corn & 1 Sack Bag d,,d }
	Robt. Moore Wagr. for Adam Rudolph}

[p. 27]

4   Cr.

1777	By amt. of Credit brought forward
June 24	By Cash 2 0 0
	By do. recd. May 28th 12 dollars
	By 2 Bushells Corn Sold Richardson
	By 10 Body Shirts
	1 Hunting Shirt
	By 4 Bushels Corn to the New Baker

Sepr. 6	By 1 Hunting Shirt to Richd. Woolton	
8	By 1 do. to Jas. Morgan	
15	By 1 do. To Danl. Thornberry	
	By the opposite 4 Bushels Corn & 1 Bag}	
May 16	deld. Saml. McColloch by Colo. Nevills}	
	order being Charged in Colo. Nevills Act.}	

[p. 28]

4

1777	To Amount brought forward Dr.		
May 29	To 2½ Bushs. Corn for Mr. Kincade p order		
June 17	To 4 Gallons vinegar	5	
	To 1 Bushel Bran	2	
	To 1½ pint of Oyl of Henry Baker	1	6
20	To 1 Sickle	7	6
	To 1 leather Cap for Negro Butt		
	To 1 Huntg. Shirt for Thos. Sewell }		
	of Capt. Walis Company }		
	To 6 sheets paper to Capt. Waggener		
	To 6 do. Capt. Lapsley		
	6 do. Capt. Walace		
	6 do. Capt. Boyer		
	6 do. Lt. Gamble		
	Forage &c Issued		
May 11	To 15 Bushs. Corn for Packhorses to Jno. Barr		
27	To 10 do. & 400wt. hay }		
	to Andw. Henry on his }		
	return from Phila. }		
16	To 4 Bushs. Corn & 1 Bag to Saml.}		
	McColloch p Colo. Nevills order}		
18	To 7 Bushs. Corn & 250wt. Hay to}		
	Jacob Blue's Team employ'd}		
	by Captn. McGuire to Carry}		
	Baggage to Dumfries }		
21	To 12 Bushels Corn for the Inocu }		

lated Soldiers to Henry Baker }
p Steenbergens order }
Amt. Carried forward

	Contra			Cr. 3
	By 100 Knapsacks	}		
	100 Hunting Shirts	}		
	58 Caps	}		
	25 Hoppesses	}	received of Mr.
	1 pair Shoes	}	Steenbergen
	2 Ovens	}	
	7 Pots	}	
	5 Axes	}	

By 2 Hunting Shirts
By ½ Bushel Corn sold Benja. Thornberry

	2 Bushels do.	to Jacob Crum
	1 do.	to Adam Anderson
	1 do.	to Isaa Sitler
	1 do.	to Chisler
	1 do.	to Strickland
June 3	2 do.	to Geo. Kyger
	4 do.	to do.
	3 do.	to Chr. Wetzle
	2 do.	to P. Hyskle
5	4 do.	to Adam Curts
	1½ do.	to Mrs. Sperry
	1 do.	to Jno. Peaton
	3 do.	to Colo. Kennedy
	2 do.	to Jos. Piles
	½ do.	to Henry Anderson
	½ do.	to Fergn. Hyland
	2 do.	to Thos. McDugal

Carried forward

[p. 30]

3

1777	To amount brought forward	Dr.	
July 14th	To 1 Hoppes for Andw. Lilburn p Mr. Routs order		
	To 1 Htg. Shirt 1 Body Shirt & 1 Hoppes for }		
	David Helms p Mr. Routs order }		
16	To 6 Iron pots & 1 duck oven} p Henry Haugh &}		
	To 12 Hoppesses & 1 Htg. Shirt} Capt. Rea's order}		
23	To 4 Body Shirts }		
	3 Hunting Shirts } p Capt. Geo. Rice		
	8 Habersacks }		
	1 Leather Cap }		
25	20 Hoppesses p Capt. Rice's order		
26	To paid Lewis Huff for Helving and } 2		
	Grinding a new ax }		
	To 2 Hunting Shirts for Mr. Smith's }		
	negro (at twice) a Waggoner }		
	To 1 Huntg. Shirt & 1 Body Shirt for Ricd. Powel}		
	To a Soldier in Capt. Waggeners Compy. }		
Mar 18	To 1 Htg. Shirt 1 Body Shirt } for Lt. }		
	1 pair Stockings } Oldham}		
	To 1 pair do. for Capt. Waggener		
	To 1 Htg. Shirt 1 Body Shirt } for Capt.		
	1 pr. Stockings }		
	Carried forwd. to Dr. side		

[p. 31]

Dr. 2

A1777	To Amount brought Forward	
Augt.	To pd. pegy Harry for makg. 7 Habersacks 10 6	
June 16	To pd. Lewis Huff for mendg. Mr.}	
	Smith's waggon } 4	
20	To 1 Bag for Saml. McCologh p Colo. }	
	Nevill's order to carry flints to Pitt }	

July 6   To 1 By. Shirt & 1 Hunting Shirt for   }
            Richd. Gibney p Mr. Rout's order   }
12th   To 2 Hoppesses for Capt. Wagr.
            1 do. For Barny Hagin
            1 do. & 1 Cap for John Smith
            1 do. & 1 do. For John McColm
            1 Body Shirt for ditto
            1 Hoppes 1 Huntg. Shirt for Jo . Littrele
            1 Cap for   do.
            1 do. & 1 Hoppes for John Buzan
            1 Body Shirt 1 Cap for Ben Sabastian
            1 Hoppes for   do.
            1 Hoppes 1 Huntg. Shirt & 1 Cap   }
                for John Demoss   }
            {p Capt. Waggeners rects.}
14   To 1 Huntg. Shirt & 1 Body Shirt   }
                for Henry Crisly p Mr.   }
            Richd. Rout's order   }

[p. 32]
2   Colo. James Wood to Achilles Foster   Dr.
1777
Apl. 10 To Cash pd. Jas. Knight for 4000wt. Hay   3   0   0
    19 To do. pd. Ed. Smith for Hay as p rect.   18   0
May 16 To do. pd. Saml. Lupton for 4000w hay
            as p do.   3   6   0
    19 To do. pd. Adam Haymaker for mindg. 2 locks 6   0
    30 To do. pd. Jas. Purviance for 36 Bundles }
            Straw for the Men in the Small Pox }   3   0
June 8   To do. pd. for 8 Galls. Tar to Sexton
            as p rect.   1   0   0
    do.To do. pd. Robert Wilson for a load Straw   1   0   0
    12 To do. pd. Henry Anderson for repairing }
            Edwd. McGuire's Stable for Wagn. }
            Horses   }   15

July 13 To pd. Wetzel for 2 Collars & Ham Strings }
    for Mr. Ed. Smiths Wagn. Horses } 1 5
A do. To pd. Wm. Campbell for Shoeg.
    Ed. Smiths Horses   4 6
Sepr. 14 To paid Timothy Wire Ratioons from the }
     24th Augt. to the 14 Sepr. & 3 days }
     allowance to go to Fredericktown }
     rations 24   }
   25 To pd. Doctr. Kayser for Timothy Wire 17 0
     To pd. ditto for Cureing Mr. Smith }
     Negro Jack a Waggoner   } 1 4

[p. 33]

    Stock to sundries   Dr.
1778   Received at the Continental Store viz
    10½ yards white Linnen
    3 yards Cloth
    1 oz Thread
    10
    1 Stick Twist
    1 pair Shoes
    ½ oz Nuns Thread
    4½ yards Strip'd Holland
    1 Stick Twist   1 oz thread
    1 dozen Small Hair Buttons
    2 larg Buttons

[p. 34]
Z   J...
   There is a receipt in the Philadelphia Magazine to make
lime hold out five times as much & make the morter much
better. The magazine may be seen by application at the new
Store in Caroline.
          Ed. Clark

[p. 35]

(Copied from MS. in possession of Walter C. Wyman, Evanston, Ill., Aug. 7, 1900.)

A Muster Roll of Capt. Harman Davis's Company of the So. Carolina Continental Regiment of Artillery command'd by Owen Roberts Esqr.   Fort Littleton, 3d. Dec. 1778.

Commssd. Officers	Ranks	Dates of Commssng.	Remarks.
Harman Davis	Captain	5 Feby. 1778	present
James Wilson	Capt. Leut.		present
James Field	First Leut.		present

Ranks	No.	Mens Names	Inlistments	What time for ye war	Remarks
Corpls.	{1	Jno. Lawrence	25 Novr. 1777	for ye war	present
	{2	Jas. Patterson	10 March 1778	3 years	Do.
Drum	3	Jno. Jones			Do.
Gunrs.	{4	Groves Doran	29 Novr. 1777	3 years	Do.
	{5	Wm. McMackin	24 Novr. 1777	3 years	Do.
	6	Jos Jno. Lockwood	29 Novr. 1777	3 years	Do.
	7	Jno. Fleming	27 Novr. 1777	3 years	Do.
	8	Jas. Hunter	27 Novr. 1777	3 years	Do.
	9	Jas. Oliphent	27 Novr. 1777	ye war	Do.
	10	Donald McDonald	15 Octobr. 1777	ye war	Do.

11	Jos. Turner	25 Novr. 1777	ye war	Do.
12	Peter Rabelais	15 Octobr. 1777	ye war	Do.
13	Jno. Stanford	1 Octobr. 1777	ye war	Do.
14	Anthony Mart	7 June, 1778	3 years	Do.
15	Charles Taylor	3 Augt. 1778	3 years	Do.

[p. 36]

Proof.

Ranks	Captain	Capt. Leut	First Leut	Sergt	Corpl	Drum	Gunners	Matrosses
Present	1	1	1	"	2	1	2	10
Absent	"	"	"	"	"	"	"	"
Totals	1	1	1	"	2	1	2	10

I do swear the within Muster Roll is a true State of the Company without fraud to the United States or any Individual according to my knoledge

Harn. Davis

Sworn before me }
this 3rd December 1778 }
    Andrew Aggnew J. P.
    State of South Carolina
        Beaufort 3d Decr. 1778

Then Mustered as Certified by
F. Bremar, Depty. Muster Master

[p. 37]
(Copied, from MS. in possession of Walter C. Wyman, Evanston, Ill., Aug. 7, 1900.)
A Muster Roll of Capt. Harman Davis's Company of the South Carolina Conl. Corps of Artillery
Commanded by Coll. Owen Roberts at Head Quarters, Purysburgh 19th March, 1779.

Commissd. Officers	Rank	Dates of Commission	Remarks.
Harman Davis.	Captain	Sixth day of Jany. 78	Present
James Wilson	Capt. Lieut.		Recruiting
James Field	Lieut.		Absent with leave

Rank	No	Mens Names	Inlistments	What time of service	Remarks
Serjeant	1	Lewis Linder	24th Novr. 1777	War	Present
Drummer	2	John Jones		War	Do.
Gunner	3	Willm. McMacken	24th Novr. 1777	3 years	Abst. on Guard
{	4	James Oliphant	27th Novr. 1777	War	Do.
{	5	James Hunter	27th Novr. 1777	3 years	Present
{	6	Joseph Turner	25th Novr. 1777	War	Abst. On Guard

Harn. Davis Capt.

Sworn before me }
the 19 March 1779 }
    J. Wise

State of South Carolina }
Head Quarters, Purysburgh }
19th March 1779. }
    Then mustered, as Certified by
        F. Bremar
        Depty. Muster Master.

INDEXING NOTE

Pages 6-14 of this volume comprise a list of American officers held as prisoners of war (POWs) by the British at Charleston, S. C., in 1780. These are identified in the manuscript only by surname and rank. Where a given name could be determined with reasonable probability from other sources, it is included in the index in square brackets; prisoners are also identified in the index with the designation (POW).

INDEX

M

www.ingramcontent.com/pod-product-compliance
Lightning Source LLC
Chambersburg PA
CBHW070753050426
42449CB00010B/2450